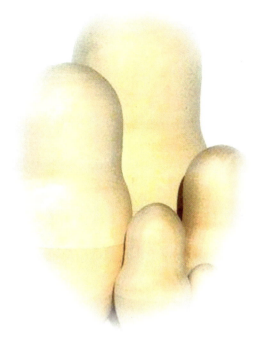

Paint your Own Nesting Dolls

Twelve Step-by-Step Projects for Decorating Blank Wooden Dolls

Carmen Barros

Introduction

I have always admired the Russian art of matryoshka or nesting dolls. A few years ago, I decided to try painting my own nesting dolls — and a satisfying hobby was born.

When I began decorating these wonderful folk art treasures, I searched for a guide that would provide basic instructions on how to paint the dolls and could not find one. I have assembled this book to assist you in creating your own nesting dolls.

Nesting dolls consist of hand carved wooden dolls, in decreasing sizes, placed one inside the other. They make wonderful decorations and gifts. The dolls can be painted simply or they can be quite elaborate.

About the Author

Carmen Barros has been involved in arts and crafts her entire life. She enjoys decorative painting and cross-stitching and is never without an art project to fill her spare time. In addition to decorating nesting dolls, Carmen paints still lifes and landscapes in water soluble oils, and has recently begun studying portrait painting.

All Rights Reserved © 2013 Carmen S. Barros
No portion of this book may be copied, retransmitted, re-posted, duplicated or otherwise used without the express written approval of the author, except by a reviewer who may quote brief passages in a review.

Paint Your Own Nesting Dolls offers twelve different patterns for painting blank wooden dolls. The first project, Pink Maiden, will give you the opportunity to begin your nesting doll painting with a simple, yet charming, design.

Another easy doll to paint is the Semenov Maiden. Semenov nesting dolls are a popular Russian design. With my step-by-step instructions, you will be able to create your own version of the doll.

The designs for the other dolls include flowers, fruits, a winter scene and two Santa patterns. Most of the dolls in the book are painted on a six-inch, five-piece nesting doll set. Cathedral Maiden is painted on an eight-inch, seven-piece nesting doll set, while Khokhloma Maiden and Wild Rose Maiden are painted on 10-inch, 10-piece sets. These dolls are truly a labor of love, but I encourage you to take the time to paint them. The end result will be well worth the effort.

I dedicate this book to my family, especially my husband, Jack, who is my biggest supporter, my son, Colin, who fills my life with music, and my son, Kevin, who fills my life with laughter. And thank you to my friends and family who have graciously accepted the many home-made gifts I have given them throughout the years.

I hope you enjoy painting your nesting dolls. If you have any questions or comments you can e-mail me at nestingdolllady@gmail.com.

Happy Painting!

Carmen Barros

Table of Contents

General Instructions 6

Painting Supplies 10

Painting Techniques 12

Nesting Doll Projects:

Pink Maiden
14

Daisy Maiden
18

Semenov Maiden
22

Strawberry Maiden
26

Rose Maiden
30

Harvest Maiden
34

Santa Claus
40

Irish Santa
46

Winter Maiden
52

Cathedral Maiden
60

Khokhloma Maiden
70

Wild Rose Maiden
76

General Instructions

Blank nesting dolls can be purchased through a number of internet retailers. The most popular nesting dolls are the five piece sets, with the largest dolls being four, five or six inches tall. I find the five-piece, six-inch doll set the easiest to work with, especially if you are just beginning to paint nesting dolls. Even with this set, the smallest doll will be barely 1.5 inches tall.

Most of the dolls in the book are painted on a six-inch, five-piece nesting doll set with the exception of Cathedral Maiden, Khokhloma Maiden and Wild Rose Maiden which are painted on larger sets.

Be sure to purchase dolls that are made in Russia to guarantee that you are getting a top quality product. For information on ordering blank nesting dolls, refer to the chapter on *Painting Supplies*.

Preparing the Dolls

Good quality nesting dolls require little preparation prior to painting. Before you begin painting, open each doll and put them back together to check how they fit. If the fit is tight, lightly sand the inside top half of the doll. Remove any stickers or labels from the dolls. Place the dolls on a flat surface. If the dolls wobble, sand the bottoms lightly to even them out. While you are painting, you will keep each doll closed (the top and bottom halves together). The insides of the dolls are not painted.

Painting the Dolls

The simplest nesting doll has a face, scarf and dress. Many dolls also have a medallion or

Nesting Dolls—Painting The Background

apron on the front for creating a design. Designs can also be painted on the scarf and dress. More elaborate dolls will have arms and hands, but these are not critical to creating an enchanting doll.

Most dolls are painted with round faces. I use a template for outlining the face on each doll. In general your tallest doll (the six inch) will have a face that is two inches in diameter; the next one a 1½ inch face; the third a 1 inch face; the fourth a ¾ inch face and the smallest a ½ inch face. These measurements, however, are approximate. Since nesting dolls are hand carved, their sizes will vary and your largest doll can range anywhere from 5¾ to 6¼ inches in height. Each doll's face, therefore, should be approximately one-third the overall size of the doll.

Begin by tracing or drawing the basic elements on each doll — the face, the scarf and the medallion. Paint each section with two to three coats of paint. Sand lightly in between each coat, if needed, to remove any ridges or bumps. Allow the paint to dry thoroughly in between coats.

At this point I separate each doll to "break" the seal created by the paints. After you separate the dolls, check them carefully to make sure there is no damage to the paint near the seams. If necessary, repair any damage. Reassemble the dolls making sure you realign the scarf and medallion patterns correctly.

Transferring the Designs

You are now ready to transfer or draw the patterns and designs onto the dolls. Dolls can have a variety of decors – flowers, scenes, animals and patterns. The possibilities are endless. However, each set of dolls will have a common theme.

Nesting Dolls – Painting the Designs

The tallest doll will have the largest and most detailed design. As the dolls become smaller, the designs become simpler. The smallest doll in a set will include just a few of the main design elements. For example if you paint daisies on your dolls, the largest doll will have several daisies in various colors. The smallest doll in the set will have only one small daisy on its belly.

In general, the patterns provided for each nesting doll set is for the largest doll in the set. To obtain the design for each subsequent doll, copy the image at 75% on a photocopier. For example, the 4½ inch doll's pattern will be 75% of the original design. The next doll's pattern will be 75% of that and so on.

Next cut out each design and using a pastel pencil rub the back of the design with a thin layer of color making sure to cover all pattern lines. Tape the paper on the doll and lightly trace over the design to transfer it to your doll. I typically transfer the main designs for each doll using the method described above, but draw the other embellishments, such as C-strokes, dots, crosshatching, etc., freehand.

Painting the Designs

Begin by painting the largest design areas first — the medallion and scarf patterns. Next, add the details, such as lace around the scarf. Paint the various designs on the doll with one to two coats of paint.

After you have painted the designs on each doll, you will paint the faces. The most important aspect of creating pleasing faces is to ensure that the eyes, nose and mouth are in the correct proportions.

To obtain the correct placement for each part

Sample Nesting Doll Faces

of the face, divide the face in half. The half way point is where you will place the eyes. Next divide the bottom half of the circle in half again. This is where the base of the nose will be. The lips are painted between the bottom of the nose and the chin.

I draw the face and hair on each doll lightly in pencil, so no two of my dolls ever look exactly alike. But if you prefer you can transfer the face designs provided using the pastel pencil method.

Completing Your Dolls

Once you have finished painting the nesting dolls, check them carefully and correct any mistakes. Don't forget to sign and date your work. I usually do this on the bottom of the largest doll.

Allow the dolls to dry completely for 24 hours. After the dolls dry, you are ready to apply the final coats of varnish to your dolls.

Separate each doll prior to varnishing them. You will only be varnishing the outside of each doll. The inside is left unpainted and unvarnished. Apply two to three thin coats of varnish, allowing the varnish to dry completely between coats.

Place the bottom half of each doll upside down to dry. I dry the top half of each doll on a drying stand which I create using old brushes inserted in the brush holes of my water basin. After you apply the final coat, let the sections dry overnight.

Once the varnish is dry, re-assemble the dolls and admire your masterpiece. Enjoy!

The Finished Dolls

Painting Supplies

Blank Nesting Dolls

The following retailer is a good source for purchasing the blank wooden nesting dolls used in this book:

Golden Cockerel
1651 NC Highway 194 North
Boone, NC 28607
1.800.892.5409
www.goldencockerel.com

Paints

The dolls in this guide are painted with craft acrylic paints. I use Plaid FolkArt®, Delta Ceramcoat® and DecoArt® paints. I thin my acrylic paints with plain water, but you can use clear medium if you prefer. The colors needed to paint each doll are listed with the project's instructions.

Once you have finished decorating your dolls, you will want to varnish them with a clear gloss. I use DecoArt® DuraClear Varnish Gloss. Apply two to three thin coats of varnish, allowing the varnish to dry completely between coats.

Brushes

You will need a selection of small paint brushes to decorate the dolls. I recommend purchasing the best quality brushes you can afford. I purchase my flat, filbert and round brushes from www.artistsclub.com. Their Papillon brushes are reasonably priced and very durable. The monogram liner brushes I recommend are manufactured by the Princeton Art & Brush Co. You should be able to find these at your local craft store.

You will need at least one each of the following sizes:

- Flat sizes #2, #4, #6, and #8
- Filbert sizes #2, #4 and #6
- Round sizes #3/10, #1 and #2
- Monogram brush size #20/0 and #10/0
- Glaze brush 1/2"

The flat brushes are used to paint the larger parts of the dolls — the scarves, dresses and medallions. Use the #6 or #8 brushes to apply color to the largest doll, the #4 or #6 brushes for the next three dolls and the #2 or #4 for the smallest one.

Use the filbert and smaller flat brushes for painting the designs. Filbert brushes are great for painting flower petals, the smaller flat brushes are useful for painting leaves and other details.

The round and monogram brushes are used for all fine linework and for painting the smaller details.

The 1/2" glaze brush is used to apply the final coats of varnish to the dolls.

Pastel Pencils

You will need one dark (blue or black) and one light (white or yellow) pastel pencil to transfer the designs to the nesting dolls. You will use the dark pencil to transfer designs onto a light background and light pencil onto a dark background. I use General's Pastel Chalk Pencil. You should be able to purchase these at your local craft store.

Paint Palette

I use a wet palette to keep my acrylic paints from drying out while I paint the dolls. Most likely you will not finish your dolls in one painting session, so a wet palette will keep your paints moist and usable for days. I recommend Masterson Sta-Wet Palette. The palette can be purchased at most local craft stores. It is available in various sizes and comes with palette paper and a sponge. You pre-moisten the palette paper and place it on top of the sponge which is fully saturated with water. You place your paints on the palette paper so they will retain their proper consistency as you paint. You can also use the paper to mix and blend your colors.

Water Basin

You will also need a basin for water to clean your brushes and thin your paints. I use the Loew Cornell® Brush Tub. The tub has two wells and holes to place your brushes in when not in use.

Sanding Sponge

To sand the dolls before painting, use very fine grit sandpaper. I use a 3M sanding sponge (fine) to even out any ridges or bumps in the paint as needed.

Templates

To draw the faces on the dolls I use a template. The Pickett Circle Master No. 12041 Inking Template is very flexible and you can use it directly on the dolls to create the outline of the faces. The template includes all the sizes you will need for your doll faces.

You can draw the medallions for each doll freehand or use a template. A good template for creating ovals is the Fiskars Ovals #4851. This template, however, is not very flexible so I use it to draw the outline for the medallions on my tracing paper. I then create the design in the medallion and transfer the pattern to the dolls.

Dot Tools

You can use the handle tips of your brushes to create dots. Another great tool for painting dots is EZ Dotz™. You can purchase it from your local craft store or order on line at www.ezdotz.com.

Painting Techniques

You will use a variety of basic brush strokes and techniques to paint the dolls. Following are definitions of some of the techniques used in this book. If you are a beginning painter, I would encourage you to purchase a book on basic brush stroke techniques and use it as a reference.

To paint the basic elements of the dolls — the scarf, dress, medallion and face — you should use paint at the consistency that it comes out of the bottle.

To paint the designs, you will want to thin the paint slightly with plain water or clear medium. For linework, the paint should be thinned to the consistency of ink.

Base or Paint

To base or paint means to apply two to three coats of paint to the surface. You will definitely need to paint the basic elements with several coats of paint. The details, such as flowers, buildings, trees, will need one to two coats of paint depending on the opacity of the color you are using.

Shading / Highlighting

You will use shading and highlighting to add depth and brightness to the designs. To shade select a color that is darker than the main color and thin it to an inky consistency. Dip one corner of your brush in the shade color and the other in plain water. Blend on your palette. Stroke your brush lightly over the area to be shaded. Allow the paint to dry and repeat if necessary.

To highlight you will use the same technique as above but with a color that is lighter than the main color. For both techniques it is best to apply the paint sparingly and repeat the process until you have the desired effect.

Brush Mix or Double-Load

Most of the flowers and leaves in this guide are painted with a double-loaded or brush mixed technique. For either technique, load each side of your brush with a different color. For the double-loaded technique blend the colors softly on your palette before applying to your design. For the brush mix technique you apply the paint directly from the brush to the surface and blend as you paint.

Dots and Dot Daisies

To get nicely round dots make sure you use fresh paint. To create even-sized dots dip your tool in the puddle of paint as you create each dot. To create progressively smaller dots, dip your tool in the puddle of paint once and create the dots without reloading. The dots will get smaller as you go. Dot daisies are created by painting a center dot with one color and surrounded it with five smaller dots of another color.

C-Strokes

C-strokes or half circle strokes are versatile techniques for painting flowers and creating lace patterns. To paint a flower with a C-stroke double-load a flat brush with paint and place the chisel edge on the surface. Apply pressure as you turn your brush to complete a half circle.

To create the C-strokes for the scarf and medallion designs, use a liner brush filled with paint thinned to an inky consistency.

Cross-hatching

Cross-hatching is used to create a mesh-like pattern. To create cross-hatching draw a series of thin, parallel lines in the design area. Cross these lines with another set of parallel lines placed at a right angle to the original lines.

Stipple or Pounce

Stippling or pouncing creates an open, textured effect. This technique is useful for painting foliage and areas where you don't want a solid coverage. To stipple or pounce load a filbert brush with a small amount of paint and blot on a paper towel. Hold the brush at a 90° angle and touch it quickly to the surface in a pouncing motion.

Wash or Glaze

Glazes are created by mixing a large amount of water with a little bit of paint. Fill your brush with the mixture, blot on a paper towel and apply lightly to the surface. Let dry and repeat if necessary. As with shading and highlighting, apply the glaze sparingly and repeat the process until you have the desired effect.

Float

Float is used primarily to add glitter paint to the various design elements. Dip your brush in the glitter paint and blot it on a paper towel. Stroke your brush lightly over the area to be painted. Repeat if necessary.

Painting Techniques

Pink Maiden

Pink Maiden is a simple design, and even if you are a beginning painter, you will be able to create your first set of nesting dolls easily. The dolls are decorated with one color and the details added with complementary ones. I have painted the dolls both with and without the braid. If you decide not to add the braid, you can center the flower in each medallion or just add another smaller flower.

Palette
FolkArt® Acrylic Paints

- Alizarin Crimson
- Fresh Foliage
- Licorice
- Light Flesh
- Medium Flesh
- Porcelain Blue
- Raw Sienna
- Real Brown
- Rose Pink
- Rose White
- Sap Green
- School Bus Yellow
- Sunflower
- Yellow Ochre
- Warm White
- Wicker White

Painting Surface
6-inch, 5-piece Blank Wooden Nesting Doll.

Brushes and Other Supplies

- Flat sizes #2, #4, #6, and #8
- Filbert sizes #1, #2 and #4
- Round sizes #3/10, #1 and #2
- Liner size #20/0 and #10/0
- Glaze brush 1/2"
- Masterson Sta-Wet Palette
- Water Basin
- Sanding Paper and Sponge
- Circle and Oval Templates
- DecoArt® Dura Clear Varnish Gloss

Preparation
Follow the directions in *General Instructions* to prepare your dolls for painting. Using the template, draw the face on each doll. As you paint, refer to the color photographs of the dolls.

Paint the Background
Paint the doll faces Light Flesh. Paint the rest of the dolls Rose Pink. Let dry.

Trace or transfer the pattern for the scarf and medallion. With Rose White outline the bottom of the scarf with a series of C-strokes. Add dots along the strokes as indicated in the pattern.

Outline the border of the medallion with Rose White. Add dots around the border of the medallion with Rose White. Add clusters of three dots around the bottom lip of the 6-inch doll with Rose White.

Medallion

Trace or transfer the flowers on each medallion. Paint the leaves with a brush mix of Sap Green and Fresh Foliage. Add soft highlights with a mix of Fresh Foliage and Sunflower.

Base each flower petal Rose White. Paint the center Rose Pink. Create a shadow on the bottom of each petal (near the flower center) with a mix of Rose Pink and Rose White. Add thin strokes on each petal with Rose Pink and Alizarin Crimson. Add dots around the center of each flower with Alizarin Crimson and Rose White.

Hair and Braid

Transfer or draw the pattern for each doll's hair and braid. Paint the hair and braid Yellow Ochre. Add streaks of Raw Sienna and Real Brown to the hair and braid. Paint a small band near the bottom of the braid with Rose Pink.

Dot Daisies

Paint small daisies around the main flower. The daisies are created by painting a dot of

School Bus Yellow, surrounded by five smaller dots of Wicker White. Add small daisies randomly on the back of each doll's scarf.

Faces

Transfer or draw the face onto each doll. Base the eyes Warm White mixed with a touch of Porcelain Blue. Shadow the top of each eye with a mix of Light Flesh and Medium Flesh. Outline the top of the eye with Real Brown and the bottom with Raw Sienna. Paint the irises Porcelain Blue and the pupils Licorice. Add a tiny dot of Wicker White to the upper right corner of each iris. Paint the eyelashes and eyebrows Real Brown. Paint two small dots for the nose Real Brown.

Paint the lips Alizarin Crimson. Draw a thin line with Licorice to delineate the top and bottom lip. Add a highlight with Wicker White on the lower lip. Add a touch of blush on the cheeks with a mix of Light Flesh and Rose Pink.

Completing your Dolls

Follow the directions in *General Instructions* for varnishing your dolls.

Pattern for Pink Maiden

Pattern may be hand traced or photocopied for personal use only. Pattern shown is for the six-inch doll. To obtain the pattern for each subsequent doll, copy the image at 75% on a photocopier. For example, the 4 and 1/2 inch doll's pattern will be 75% of the original design. The next doll's pattern will be 75% of that and so on.

Daisy Maiden

Like most nesting dolls, Daisy Maiden is painted with a different color for the scarf and dress. You can easily change the colors and create a totally different doll. I have painted the dolls with a pink scarf and blue dress, or with a darker and lighter version of the same color for the scarf and dress. You can also change the colors of the daisies to coordinate with your background color.

Palette

FolkArt® Acrylic Paints

- Berry Wine
- Fresh Foliage
- Licorice
- Light Flesh
- Medium Flesh
- Porcelain Blue
- Prussian Blue
- Raw Sienna
- Real Brown
- Rose Pink
- Sap Green
- School Bus Yellow
- Yellow Ochre
- Warm White
- Wicker White

Painting Surface

6-inch, 5-piece Blank Wooden Nesting Doll.

Brushes and Other Supplies

- Flat sizes #2, #4, #6, and #8
- Filbert sizes #1, #2 and #4
- Round sizes #3/10, #1 and #2
- Liner size #20/0 and #10/0
- Glaze brush 1/2"
- Masterson Sta-Wet Palette
- Water Basin
- Sanding Paper and Sponge
- Circle and Oval Templates
- DecoArt® Dura Clear Varnish Gloss

Preparation

Follow the directions in *General Instructions* to prepare your dolls for painting. Using the template, draw the face on each doll. Transfer or draw the outline for each doll's scarf. As you paint, refer to the color photographs of the dolls.

Paint the Background

Paint the doll faces Light Flesh. Paint the scarf of the four largest dolls Porcelain Blue. Paint the dress Rose Pink. The smallest doll is painted Porcelain Blue. Let dry.

Hair and Braid

Transfer or draw the pattern for each doll's hair and braid. Paint the hair Yellow Ochre. Add streaks of Raw Sienna and Real Brown to the hair and braid.

Paint the bow on the braid with a mix of Rose Pink and Wicker White. Shade the inside of the bow with Rose Pink. Outline the bow with thinned Wicker White.

Scarf and Dress Detail

Paint the bottom of the scarf with C-strokes and small dots using Wicker White.

Paint the lace around each doll's face with double C-strokes and small dots with Wicker White. Use Wicker White to paint a series of interlocking C-strokes on the bottom rim of the 6-inch doll.

Add random groups of three dots to the dress with School Bus Yellow.

Daisies

Transfer the pattern for the daisies to each doll. Daisies are painted Berry Wine or Prussian Blue double-loaded with Wicker White. Paint the center of each daisy School Bus Yellow. Add tiny black and white dots around the yellow center of each daisy. Outline the daisy petals with thinned Wicker White.

Paint the leaves with a brush mix of Sap Green and Fresh Foliage. Outline each leaf with thinned School Bus Yellow.

Randomly place dot daisies on each doll's scarf. These daisies have a center dot of School Bus Yellow surrounded by five dots of Wicker White.

Faces

Transfer or draw the face onto each doll. Base the eyes Warm White mixed with a touch of Porcelain Blue. Shadow the top of each eye with a mix of Light Flesh and Medium Flesh. Outline the top of the eye Real Brown and the bottom Raw Sienna.

Paint the irises Porcelain Blue and the pupils Licorice. Add a tiny dot of Wicker White to the upper right corner of each iris. Paint the eyelashes and eyebrows Real Brown.

Paint the lips Berry Wine. Draw a thin line with Licorice to delineate the top and bottom lip. Add a highlight with Wicker White on the lower lip.

Outline the nose with a mix of Light Flesh and Rose Pink. Add two small dots with Real Brown.

Add a touch of blush on the cheeks with a mix of Light Flesh and Rose Pink.

Completing your Dolls

Follow the directions in *General Instructions* for varnishing your dolls.

Pattern for Daisy Maiden

Pattern may be hand traced or photocopied for personal use only. Pattern shown is for the six-inch doll. To obtain the pattern for each subsequent doll, copy the image at 75% on a photocopier. For example, the 4 and 1/2 inch doll's pattern will be 75% of the original design. The next doll's pattern will be 75% of that and so on.

Semenov Maiden

The Semenov Maiden is a popular Russian design. The dolls originate in the town of Semenov in western Russia. They are known for their colorful bouquet of flowers and distinctive yellow scarves.

Palette
FolkArt® Acrylic Paints
- Christmas Red
- Fresh Foliage
- Lemonade
- Licorice
- Light Flesh
- Medium Flesh
- Porcelain Blue
- Raw Sienna
- Real Brown
- Rose Pink
- Sap Green
- Warm White
- Wicker White

Painting Surface
6-inch, 5-piece Blank Wooden Nesting Doll.

Brushes and Other Supplies
- Flat sizes #2, #4, #6, and #8
- Filbert sizes #1, #2 and #4
- Round sizes #3/10, #1 and #2
- Liner size #20/0 and #10/0
- Glaze brush 1/2"
- Masterson Sta-Wet Palette
- Water Basin
- Sanding Paper and Sponge
- Circle and Oval Templates
- DecoArt® Dura Clear Varnish Gloss

Preparation
Follow the directions in *General Instructions* to prepare your dolls for painting. Using the template, draw the face on each doll. Transfer or draw the outline for each doll's scarf and medallion. As you paint, refer to the color photographs of the dolls.

Paint the Background
Paint the doll faces Light Flesh. Paint the scarf and bow of each doll Lemonade and the dress Christmas Red. Paint the medallions Wicker White. Let dry.

Medallion Design
Transfer the rose design to the medallion. Paint the leaves Sap Green. Highlight with Fresh Foliage.

Paint the roses Christmas Red. Create the details on each rose with Licorice. Outline the leaves with Licorice.

Scarf
Transfer the pattern for the roses to the scarf of each doll. The roses on the scarf are painted the same as those on the medallion.

Create a border on the scarf with Licorice. Add tiny rose buds with Christmas Red and small leaves with Fresh Foliage. Create the details on the rose buds with Licorice. Outline the bow with Licorice.

Paint swirls with a liner brush and thinned Licorice on the scarf and dress of each doll.

Faces

Transfer or draw the face on each doll. Paint the hair Real Brown. Darken with a wash of thinned Licorice.

Base the eyes Warm White mixed with a touch of Porcelain Blue. Shadow the top of each eye with a mix of Light Flesh and Medium Flesh. Outline the top of the eye Real Brown and the bottom of the eye Raw Sienna.

Paint the irises Raw Sienna and the pupils Licorice. Add a tiny dot of Wicker White to the upper right corner of each iris. Paint the eyelashes and eyebrows using Real Brown.

Outline the nose with a mix of Light Flesh and Rose Pink. Add two small dots with Real Brown.

Paint the lips Christmas Red. Add small round circles of blush on the cheeks with a mix of Light Flesh and Rose Pink.

Completing your Dolls
Follow the directions in *General Instructions* for varnishing your dolls.

Pattern for Semenov Maiden

Pattern may be hand traced or photocopied for personal use only. Pattern shown is for the six-inch doll. To obtain the pattern for each subsequent doll, copy the image at 75% on a photocopier. For example, the 4 and 1/2 inch doll's pattern will be 75% of the original design. The next doll's pattern will be 75% of that and so on.

Strawberry Maiden

 Strawberry Maiden would look wonderful decorating a kitchen counter. You can easily change the dolls' colors to ones that coordinate with your décor.

Palette
FolkArt® Acrylic Paints
- Alizarin Crimson
- Fresh Foliage
- Italian Sage
- Lemonade
- Licorice
- Light Flesh
- Medium Flesh
- Medium Orange
- Olive Green
- Porcelain Blue
- Raw Sienna
- Real Brown
- Rose Pink
- Sap Green
- School Bus Yellow
- True Burgundy
- Warm White

Painting Surface
6-inch, 5-piece Blank Wooden Nesting Doll.

Brushes and Other Supplies
- Flat sizes #2, #4, #6, and #8
- Filbert sizes #1, #2 and #4
- Round sizes #3/10, #1 and #2
- Liner size #20/0 and #10/0
- Glaze brush 1/2"
- Masterson Sta-Wet Palette
- Water Basin
- Sanding Paper and Sponge
- Circle and Oval Templates
- DecoArt® Dura Clear Varnish Gloss

Preparation
Follow the directions in *General Instructions* to prepare your dolls for painting. Using the template, draw the face on each doll. Transfer or draw the outline for each doll's scarf and medallion. As you paint, refer to the color photographs of the dolls.

Paint the Background
Paint the doll faces Light Flesh. Paint the scarf of each doll Italian Sage and the dress Olive Green. Paint the medallion Warm White. Let dry.

Medallion Design
Transfer the strawberry design to the belly. Base the leaves Sap Green. Highlight with Fresh Foliage and Lemonade.

Working on one berry at a time paint the strawberries True Burgundy. While the paint is still wet, pick up Alizarin Crimson and add to one side of the berry. Pick up Medium Orange and a touch of Warm White and add to opposite side of the berry. Blend softly. Add thin strokes of Warm White and small dots of Licorice to create the strawberry seeds.

Scarf and Dress Details

Paint the lace and bow around the face Olive Green.

Use Warm White to paint the details on the lace, scarf and dress. The lace design is created using C-strokes, cross hatching and dots. Use C-strokes to create the design around the medallion. Outline the bottom edge of the scarf with a row of evenly spaced dots. Create the fringe on the bottom of the scarf with progressively smaller dots. Paint the scroll pattern on the bottom of the 6-inch doll's dress.

Flowers and Butterfly

Transfer the pattern for the daisies to the medallion and scarf. Paint the leaves Sap Green. Highlight with Fresh Foliage and Lemonade.

Paint the flowers Lemonade. Add a wash of thinned Warm White to brighten each daisy. Paint the center School Bus Yellow. Use Sap Green to outline each daisy, add the strokes on the petals and the dots around the center. Add random groups of three dots around the flowers with Warm White.

Base the butterfly Lemonade. To create shadows, add a wash of thinned School Bus Yellow around the edges of the wings. Paint the pattern on the wings with Licorice.

Faces

Transfer or draw the face on each doll. Paint

the hair Raw Sienna. Highlight with Real Brown and Licorice.

Paint the eyes Warm White mixed with a touch of Porcelain Blue. Shadow the top of each eye with a mix of Light Flesh and Medium Flesh. Outline the top of the eye Real Brown and the bottom of the eye Raw Sienna.

Paint the irises Raw Sienna and the pupils Licorice. Add a tiny dot of Warm White to the upper right corner of each iris. Paint the eyelashes and eyebrows Real Brown.

Outline the nose with a mix of Light Flesh and Rose Pink. Add two small dots with Real Brown.

Paint the lips Alizarin Crimson. Draw a thin line with Licorice to delineate the top and bottom lip. Add a highlight with Wicker White on the lower lip. Add a touch of blush on the cheeks with a mix of Light Flesh and Rose Pink.

Completing your Dolls

Follow the directions in *General Instructions* for varnishing your dolls.

Pattern for Strawberry Maiden

Pattern may be hand traced or photocopied for personal use only. Pattern shown is for the six-inch doll. To obtain the pattern for each subsequent doll, copy the image at 75% on a photocopier. For example, the 4 and 1/2 inch doll's pattern will be 75% of the original design. The next doll's pattern will be 75% of that and so on.

Rose Maiden

Rose Maiden makes a charming gift for a little girl. The roses are simple to paint. They are painted in a solid color. The details are added with a highlight color.

Palette

FolkArt® Acrylic Paints
- Berry Wine
- Dioxazine Purple
- Fresh Foliage
- Icy White
- Lavender
- Lemonade
- Light Flesh
- Medium Flesh
- Raw Sienna
- Real Brown
- Rose Pink
- Sap Green
- Warm White
- Wicker White

Delta Ceramcoat® Acrylic Paints
- Dark Night Blue
- Wedgewood Blue

Painting Surface
6-inch, 5-piece Blank Wooden Nesting Doll.

Brushes and Other Supplies
- Flat sizes #2, #4, #6, and #8
- Filbert sizes #1, #2 and #4
- Round sizes #3/10, #1 and #2
- Liner size #20/0 and #10/0
- Glaze brush 1/2"
- Masterson Sta-Wet Palette
- Water Basin
- Sanding Paper and Sponge
- Circle and Oval Templates
- DecoArt® Dura Clear Varnish Gloss

Preparation
Follow the directions in *General Instructions* to prepare your dolls for painting. Using the template, draw the face on each doll. Transfer or draw the outline for each doll's scarf and medallion. As you paint, refer to the color photographs of the dolls.

Paint the Background
Paint the doll faces Light Flesh. Paint the scarf of the four largest dolls Wedgewood Blue and the dress Dark Night Blue. Paint the medallions Icy White. Paint the top of the medallion Dark Night Blue. Paint the smallest doll Dark Night Blue and its medallion Icy White. Let dry.

Medallion Design
Transfer the rose designs to the medallion. The two largest dolls have three roses as the medallion design. The third doll has only two roses in its medallion, and the two smallest dolls have a rose bud. Paint one rose Dioxazine Purple, one Rose Pink and one Lavender. Drawn the details on each rose with Icy White. Base the leaves Sap Green. Highlight with Fresh Foliage and Lemonade.

With Wicker White paint the lace pattern on the top of the medallion. Place Wicker White dots around the medallion.

Scarf and Dress Details

Transfer the rose designs to the scarf. Paint the roses and leaves as described above.

Randomly place dot daisies throughout the scarf. These daisies have a center dot of Lemonade surrounded by five dots of Wicker White.

Paint dot daisies on the scarf around the doll's face.

With thinned Wicker White create the fringe pattern on the bottom of the scarf.

Faces

Transfer or draw the face on each doll. Base the hair with two coats of Raw Sienna. Highlight with thin strokes of Lemonade.

Base the eyes Warm White mixed with a touch of Wedgewood Blue. Shadow the top of each eye with a mix of Light Flesh and Medium Flesh. Outline the top of the eye Real Brown and the bottom Raw Sienna.

Paint the irises Wedgewood Blue and the pupils Licorice. Add a tiny dot of Wicker White to the upper right corner of each iris. Paint the eyelashes and eyebrows Real Brown.

Paint two small dots for the nose with Real Brown.

Paint the lips Berry Wine. Draw a thin line with Licorice to delineate the top and bottom lip. Add a highlight with Wicker White on the lower lip. Add a touch of blush on the cheeks with a mix of Light Flesh and Rose Pink.

Completing your Dolls

Follow the directions in *General Instructions* for varnishing your dolls.

Pattern for Rose Maiden

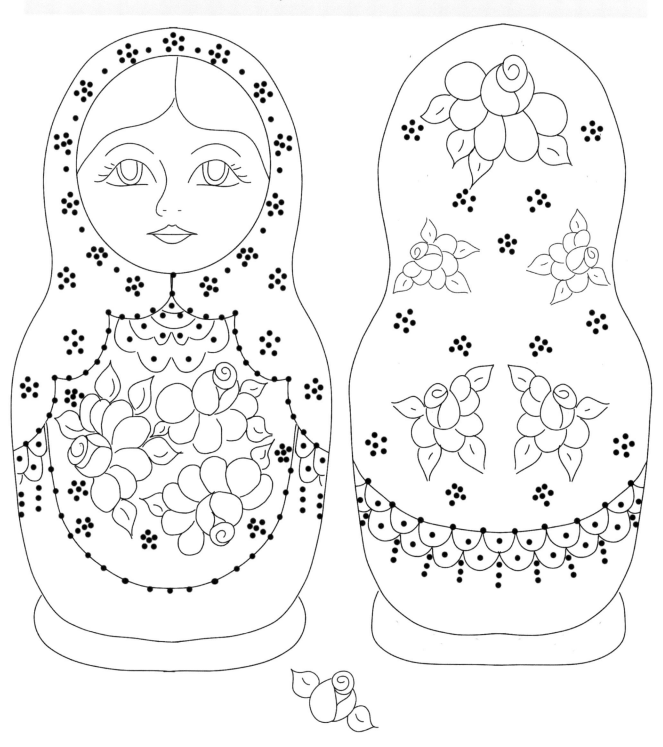

Pattern may be hand traced or photocopied for personal use only. Pattern shown is for the six-inch doll. To obtain the pattern for each subsequent doll, copy the image at 75% on a photocopier. For example, the 4 and 1/2 inch doll's pattern will be 75% of the original design. The next doll's pattern will be 75% of that and so on.

Harvest Maiden

 Harvest Maiden decorates the bookcase in my kitchen. The design is intricate but if you follow the step-by-step instructions, you will create a charming decoration for your home.

Palette

FolkArt® Acrylic Paints
- Alizarin Crimson
- Burnt Sienna
- Hauser Green Light
- Hauser Green Medium
- Licorice
- Light Flesh
- Medium Flesh
- Medium Orange
- Porcelain Blue
- Prussian Blue
- Raw Sienna
- Real Brown
- Rose Pink
- Sap Green
- School Bus Yellow
- Warm White
- Wicker White

Delta Ceramcoat® Acrylic Paints
- Christmas Red

DecoArt® Metallics
- Champagne Gold

Painting Surface
6-inch, 5-piece Blank Wooden Nesting Doll.

Brushes and Other Supplies
- Flat sizes #2, #4, #6, and #8
- Filbert sizes #1, #2 and #4
- Round sizes #3/10, #1 and #2
- Liner size #20/0 and #10/0
- Glaze brush 1/2"
- Masterson Sta-Wet Palette
- Water Basin
- Sanding Paper and Sponge
- Circle and Oval Templates
- DecoArt® Dura Clear Varnish Gloss

Preparation
Follow the directions in *General Instructions* to prepare your dolls for painting. Using the template, draw the face on each doll. Transfer or draw the outline for each doll's scarf, blouse and sleeves. As you paint, refer to the color photographs of the dolls.

Paint the Background
Paint the doll faces Light Flesh. Paint the scarf School Bus Yellow, the blouse Hauser Green Medium, the skirt Burnt Sienna and the sleeves Christmas Red. Paint the crown Champagne Gold. Let dry.

Fruit Baskets
Transfer the designs for the fruit baskets. The three larger dolls are carrying fruit baskets filled with apples. The two smaller dolls are carrying individual apples.

Paint the leaves Sap Green. Highlight with Hauser Green Light. Base the apples with one coat Medium Orange. Apply a second coat with Christmas Red. Shade the left side of each apple with Alizarin Crimson. Highlight the right side of each apple with a wash of School Bus Yellow. Add a stroke of Wicker White to each apple on the right side. Paint the stem Licorice.

Paint the baskets with a mix of Burnt Sienna and a touch of School Bus Yellow. Define the wooden slats with Licorice. Highlight random parts of the baskets with a wash of School Bus Yellow.

Hands

Trace the hands. Paint the hands Light Flesh with a touch of Alizarin Crimson. Outline the hands and fingers with Real Brown.

Sleeves

Shade the bottom of the sleeves with Alizarin Crimson. Outline the sleeves with Licorice. Add the design on the sleeves with Wicker White.

Blouse

To create the folds on the blouse select your smallest flat brush. Moisten the brush with water. Pick up a tiny bit of Sap Green on one side of the brush. Blend softly on your palette. Apply the paint lightly to create a shad-

ow for each crease. Use thinned Sap Green to darken the underside of the blouse near each crease. Paint the designs on the blouse Wicker White. Add the lace on the bottom of the blouse with small C-strokes with Wicker White.

Paint the design on the bottom rim of the largest doll with Wicker White.

Scarf

To create the folds on the scarf use the same technique described above using Medium Orange. Use thinned Medium Orange to darken the underside of the scarf near each crease. Paint the designs on the scarf with Wicker White. Decorate the scarf around the crown with small C-strokes in Wicker White.

Faces

Transfer or draw the face onto each doll. Base the eyes Warm White mixed with a touch of Porcelain Blue. Shadow the top of each eye with a mix of Light Flesh and Medium Flesh. Outline the top of the eye Burnt Sienna and the bottom Raw Sienna. Paint the irises Prussian Blue and the pupils Licorice. Add a tiny dot of Wicker White to the upper right corner of each iris. Paint the eyelashes and eyebrows Burnt Sienna.

Paint the lips Alizarin Crimson. Draw a thin line with Licorice to delineate the top and bottom lip. Add a highlight with Wicker White on the lower lip. Outline the nose with a mix of Light Flesh and Rose Pink. Add two small dots with Burnt Sienna. Add a touch of blush on the cheeks with a mix of Light Flesh and Rose Pink.

Crown

Paint the designs on the crown with Wicker White thinned to an inky consistency. The soft lace on the forehead is painted with a wash of Wicker White. Start with a small amount of Wicker White mixed with lots of water. Apply lightly to create the lace. Let dry and repeat if necessary. Create the folds in the lace with thinned Wicker White.

Earrings and Brooch

Paint the jewels on the earrings and the brooch Prussian Blue. Outline the brooch with Wicker White. Create the chain and details for the earrings with Wicker White.

Completing your Dolls

Follow the directions in *General Instructions* for varnishing your dolls.

Lace Pattern

Paint the lace with a wash of Wicker White.

Paint C-strokes and designs on crown with thinned Wicker White.

Paint the jewels on the earrings and brooch Prussian Blue.

Pattern for Harvest Maiden

Pattern may be hand traced or photocopied for personal use only. Pattern shown is for the six-inch doll. To obtain the scarf and dress pattern for each subsequent doll, copy the image at 75% on a photocopier. For example, the 4 and 1/2 inch doll's pattern will be 75% of the original design. The next doll's pattern will be 75% of that and so on. Reduce the fruit details for the 4 and 1/2 inch doll and smaller ones to 50% on a photocopier.

Pattern for Harvest Maiden

Pattern may be hand traced or photocopied for personal use only. Pattern shown is for the six-inch doll. To obtain the pattern for each subsequent doll, copy the image at 75% on a photocopier. For example, the 4 and 1/2 inch doll's pattern will be 75% of the original design. The next doll's pattern will be 75% of that and so on.

Santa Claus

A Santa Claus nesting doll will make a wonderful display for your holiday mantel.

Palette

FolkArt® Acrylic Paints
- Burnt Sienna
- Fresh Foliage
- Lemonade
- Licorice
- Light Gray
- Porcelain Blue
- Sparkles Pure Gold Glitter
- Wicker White

Delta Ceramcoat® Acrylic Paints
- Autumn Brown
- Barn Red
- Christmas Green
- Christmas Red
- Dark Night Blue
- Light Chocolate Brown
- Metallic 14K Gold
- Santa's Flesh
- Warm White

Painting Surface
6-inch, 5-piece Blank Wooden Nesting Doll.

Brushes and Other Supplies
- Flat sizes #2, #4, #6, and #8
- Filbert sizes #1, #2 and #4
- Round sizes #3/10, #1 and #2
- Liner size #20/0 and #10/0
- Glaze brush 1/2"
- Masterson Sta-Wet Palette
- Water Basin
- Sanding Paper and Sponge
- Circle and Oval Templates
- DecoArt® Dura Clear Varnish Gloss

Preparation
Follow the directions in *General Instructions* to prepare your dolls for painting. Using the template, draw the face on each of the four largest dolls. Transfer the outline for Santa's beard, hair, hat and belt. For the snowman doll transfer the outline of the hat. As you paint, refer to the color photographs of the dolls.

Paint the Background
Paint the faces of the four largest dolls Santa's Flesh. Paint the beard and hair Wicker White. Paint the hat Christmas Green and the fur Wicker White.

Paint the coat and pants of each doll Barn Red. Paint the belt (and the base of the 5-inch doll) Licorice. On each belt paint the buckle Metallic 14K Gold.

For the snowman doll paint the hat Christmas Green and the rest of the doll Wicker White. Allow to dry. Transfer the designs on the dolls.

Teddy Bear and Stocking

Paint the teddy bear Light Chocolate Brown. Load a small flat brush with a combination of Light Chocolate Brown and Autumn Brown and pounce the fur on the bear.

Pounce shadows on the inside of the ears, around the nose and on the underside of each arm with Autumn Brown. Pounce highlights on the top of the ears, head, nose and arms with a mix of Light Chocolate Brown and Wicker White.

Outline the nose and mouth with Licorice. Add a dot of Licorice for each eye. Add a smaller dot of Wicker White on each eye as a highlight.

For the bow, paint the top Fresh Foliage and the underside Christmas Green. Add shadows near the tie of the bow with Christmas Green. Float Sparkles Pure Gold Glitter on the bow.

Paint the stocking Porcelain Blue and the fur Wicker White. Pounce a blend of Wicker White and Light Gray on the fur. Shadow with thinned Dark Night Blue under the fur and down the left side of the boot. Add snowflakes with Wicker White.

Present

Paint the box Christmas Green, the top of the lid Christmas Green and the side of the lid Fresh Foliage.

Paint the top of the bow Metallic 14K Gold and the underside Burnt Sienna. Paint the ribbon Metallic 14K Gold. Add swirls to the box with Metallic 14K Gold.

Bells

Paint the bells Burnt Sienna. Highlight with Metallic 14K Gold. Paint the top of the bow Fresh Foliage and the underside Christmas Green. Float Sparkles Pure Gold Glitter on the bells and bow.

Candy Canes

Paint one candy cane Christmas Green and the other Christmas Red. Add stripes with Wicker White.

Christmas Trees

Base each Christmas tree Fresh Foliage. Add shadows on the right side of the tree with a wash of Christmas Green. Highlight on the left with a wash of Lemonade.

Paint the trunk with a blend of Light Chocolate and Autumn Brown. Add the lights and star with Metallic 14K Gold. Float Sparkles Pure Gold Glitter on each tree.

Hats

Add dots to the hats with Wicker White. Paint the small bell on each hat Burnt Sienna. Highlight with Metallic 14K Gold. Create the details on each bell with Licorice. Pounce Wicker White with a small amount of Light Gray on hat fur. Float Sparkles Pure Gold Glitter on hat, fur and bell.

Details of Santa Claus Decorations

Faces

Transfer or draw the face on each doll. Base the eyes Warm White mixed with a touch of Porcelain Blue. Outline the top of the eye Licorice and the bottom of the eye Light Chocolate Brown.

Paint the irises Porcelain Blue and the pupils Licorice. Add a tiny dot of Wicker White to the upper right corner of each iris. Paint the eyelashes Licorice.

Paint the lips Barn Red. Draw a thin line with Licorice to delineate the top and bottom lips. Add a highlight with Wicker White on the lower lip.

Paint the eyebrows and mustache Wicker White. Add individual hairs with Light Gray. Paint the nose with a mix of Santa's Flesh and a touch of Barn Red. Use the same mix to add blush on the cheeks.

Beard and Hair

For the beard and hair on each Santa, alternately add wavy stripes with Wicker White and Light Gray.

Snowman

Add small dots on the hat with Wicker White. Paint the scarf and carrot nose Barn Red. Add small stripes on the carrot nose with Licorice. Paint the eyes, mouth and buttons on the snowman with Licorice.

Completing your Dolls

Follow the directions in *General Instructions* for varnishing your dolls.

Pattern for Santa Claus

Pattern may be hand traced or photocopied for personal use only. Front pattern shown is for the six-inch doll. To obtain the back pattern for each subsequent doll, copy the image at 75% on a photocopier. For example, the 4 and 1/2 inch doll's pattern will be 75% of the original design. The next doll's pattern will be 75% of that and so on.

Pattern for Santa Claus

Pattern may be hand traced or photocopied for personal use only. Patterns shown should be the correct size for each doll but since nesting doll sizes vary you may need to adjust accordingly.

Irish Santa Claus

 If you know anyone who is Irish, this doll makes a perfect gift. I painted this doll for my son (who is half Irish) and he displays it year round.

Palette

FolkArt® Acrylic Paints
- Burnt Sienna
- Fresh Foliage
- Green Umber
- Lemonade
- Licorice
- Light Gray
- Porcelain Blue
- Sparkles Pure Gold Glitter
- Wicker White

Delta Ceramcoat® Acrylic Paints
- Autumn Brown
- Barn Red
- Dark Night Blue
- Metallic 14K Gold
- Santa's Flesh
- Warm White

Painting Surface
6-inch, 5-piece Blank Wooden Nesting Doll.

Brushes and Other Supplies
- Flat sizes #2, #4, #6, and #8
- Filbert sizes #1, #2 and #4
- Round sizes #3/10, #1 and #2
- Liner size #20/0 and #10/0
- Glaze brush 1/2"
- Masterson Sta-Wet Palette
- Water Basin
- Sanding Paper and Sponge
- Circle and Oval Templates
- DecoArt® Dura Clear Varnish Gloss

Preparation
Follow the directions in *General Instructions* to prepare your dolls for painting. Using the template, draw the face on each of the four largest dolls. Transfer the outline for Santa's hair, beard, hat and robe. For the snowman doll transfer the outline of the hat and robe. As you paint, refer to the color photographs of the dolls.

Paint the Background
Paint the faces of the four largest dolls Santa's Flesh. Use Wicker White to paint the beard, hair and the front and bottom trim of the robe. Paint the hat and robe Green Umber. Outline the sleeves on each doll with Wicker White. Paint the cuff of the sleeves Wicker White. Paint the mittens Barn Red.

For the snowman doll paint the hat and robe Green Umber and the rest of the doll Wicker White. Allow to dry. Transfer the designs on the dolls.

Bells

Base the bells Burnt Sienna. Highlight with a light coat of Metallic 14K Gold. Shadow the left side of the bells with thinned Burnt Sienna and highlight the right side with thinned Lemonade.

Paint the rim around the bottom of bells Lemonade. Paint bell clappers Autumn Brown. Float Sparkles Pure Gold Glitter on bells.

String of Lights

Paint chain and top of bulbs Delta Metallic 14K Gold. Outline with Licorice.

Paint light bulbs Porcelain Blue, Lemonade, Fresh Foliage, and Barn Red. Add a stroke of Wicker White to each bulb as a highlight. Float Sparkles Pure Gold Glitter on each bulb.

Jingle Bells

Paint bells Delta Metallic 14K Gold. Add shadow on left with thinned Burnt Sienna. Add details to bells with Burnt Sienna. Float Sparkles Pure Gold Glitter on each bell.

Pot of Gold

Base pot of gold Burnt Sienna. Highlight with Metallic 14K Gold. Paint rope Autumn Brown.

Paint gold coins Lemonade. Outline with Burnt Sienna. Float Sparkles Pure Gold Glitter on the coins.

Details on Robe and Gloves

On the three largest dolls, paint a row of shamrocks on the front of each robe with Green Umber. Add shamrocks on the sleeve cuffs of the largest doll and dots on the cuffs of the other dolls with Green Umber.

On the 5-inch doll add a series of three dots along the bottom rim with Green Umber.

Add buttons on the right and left front of each robe with Metallic 14K Gold. Add random snowflakes on sides and back of each robe with thinned Wicker White. Add the pattern on the mittens with thinned Wicker White.

Hats

Stipple the hat fur Wicker White. Float Sparkles Pure Gold Glitter on the fur.

Faces

Transfer or draw the face on each doll. Base the eyes Warm White mixed with a touch of Porcelain Blue. Outline the top of the eye Licorice and the bottom of the eye Light Chocolate Brown.

Details of Irish Santa Claus Decorations

Paint the irises Porcelain Blue and the pupils Licorice. Add a tiny dot of Wicker White to the upper right corner of each iris. Paint the eyelashes Licorice. Paint the eyebrows and mustache Wicker White. Add individual hairs with Light Gray.

Paint the lips Barn Red. Draw a thin line with Licorice to delineate the top and bottom lips. Add a highlight with Wicker White on the lower lip.

Paint the nose with a mix of Santa's Flesh and a touch of Barn Red. Use the same mix to add blush on the cheeks.

Beard and Hair

For the beard and hair on each Santa, alternately add wavy stripes with Wicker White and Light Gray.

Snowman

Add small dots on the hat with Wicker White. Add random snowflakes to the robe with Wicker White.

Paint the carrot nose Barn Red. Add small stripes on the carrot nose with Licorice. Paint the eyes, mouth and buttons with Licorice.

Completing your Dolls

Follow the directions in *General Instructions* for varnishing your dolls.

Pattern for Irish Santa Claus

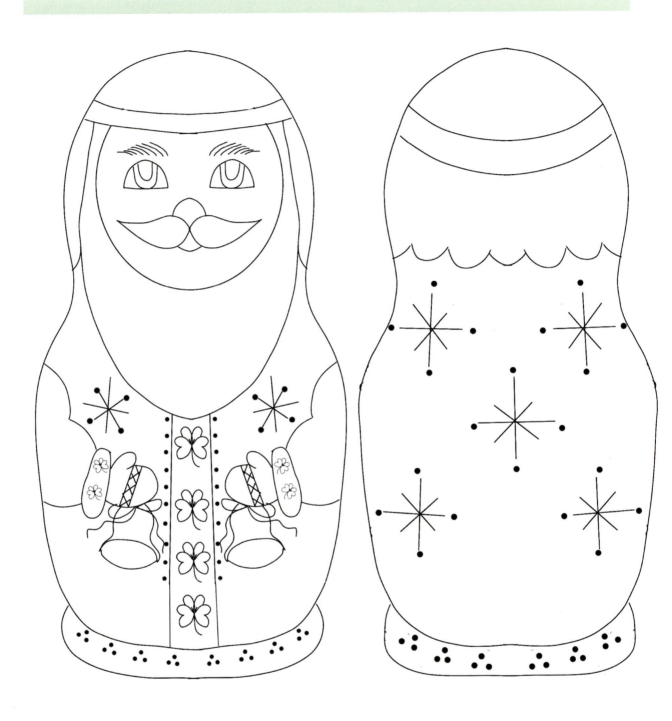

Pattern may be hand traced or photocopied for personal use only. Front pattern shown is for the six-inch doll. To obtain the back pattern for each subsequent doll, copy the image at 75% on a photocopier. For example, the 4 and 1/2 inch doll's pattern will be 75% of the original design. The next doll's pattern will be 75% of that and so on.

Pattern for Irish Santa Claus

Pattern may be hand traced or photocopied for personal use only. Patterns shown should be the correct size for each doll but since nesting doll sizes vary you may need to adjust accordingly.

Winter Maiden

I have painted Winter Maiden many times and given the dolls as gifts to family and friends. The design can easily be adapted for a larger nesting doll set.

Palette

FolkArt® Acrylic Paints
- Alizarin Crimson
- Burnt Sienna
- Fresh Foliage
- Icy White
- Lemonade
- Licorice
- Light Flesh
- Light Gray
- Medium Flesh
- Medium Orange
- Porcelain Blue
- Prussian Blue
- Real Brown
- Rose Pink
- Sap Green
- Warm White
- Wicker White
- Wrought Iron

Delta Ceramcoat® Acrylic Paints
- Dark Night Blue

DecoArt®
- Craft Twinkles Gold
- Splendid Gold

Painting Surface
6-inch, 5-piece Blank Wooden Nesting Doll.

Brushes and Other Supplies
- Flat sizes #2, #4, #6, and #8
- Filbert sizes #1, #2 and #4
- Round sizes #3/10, #1 and #2
- Liner size #20/0 and #10/0
- Glaze brush 1/2"
- Masterson Sta-Wet Palette
- Water Basin
- Sanding Paper and Sponge
- Circle and Oval Templates
- DecoArt® Dura Clear Varnish Gloss

Preparation
Follow the directions in *General Instructions* to prepare your dolls for painting. Using the template, draw the face on each doll. Transfer or draw the outline for each doll's scarf and medallion. As you paint, refer to the color photographs of the dolls.

Paint the Background
Paint the doll faces Light Flesh. Paint the scarf of the four largest dolls Splendid Gold and the dress Prussian Blue. Paint the medallions Icy White. Add evenly spaced groupings of three dots around the bottom of the six-inch doll with Warm White. Paint the smallest doll Prussian Blue. Paint her crown Splendid Gold. Let dry.

Medallion Background

Transfer the pattern for the moon, mountains and river onto each medallion.

With Dark Night Blue begin painting the sky at the top. Without cleaning the brush pick up some Icy White and continue filling in the sky. The sky should gradually become lighter as you get closer to the horizon. Allow to dry.

Paint the moon with a mix of Lemonade and Warm White. Add a thin wash of Lemonade on about half of the moon. Add streaks of Icy White to create a cloudy sky being careful not to completely cover the dark night color. Add small dots to the sky area with Warm White to create snowflakes.

With Warm White paint the mountains and snow covered fields. Add touches of Light Gray and Icy White to the Warm White to create shadows in the snow.

Paint the river Dark Night Blue. Without cleaning the brush, pick up Icy White and lighten the top portion of the river. Add streaks of Icy White to suggest ice patches on the river.

Detail of medallion on six-inch doll.

Allow the medallions to dry. Transfer pattern for the buildings, trees and other details.

Buildings

Paint each building Burnt Sienna, the windows Lemonade and the roofs Warm White. Shade the sides of each building (which is away from the moonlight) with a mix of Burnt Sienna and Real Brown. Add the wooden slats on each building with Real Brown.

Add a touch of Medium Orange on the top and left side of each window to create a soft glow. Paint all windows slats Real Brown. (Do not add the slats in the picture window of the home on the six-inch doll. You will add these after you paint the Christmas tree.)

Double load a small brush with Burnt Sienna and Real Brown and paint a chimney on each building .

Apply another coat of Warm White to the roofs and, while the paint is still wet, add touches of Light Gray and Icy White to create shadows. Pounce snow on the top or bottom of each window and the top of each chimney with Warm White. Add wisps of smoke with Light Gray coming from each chimney.

Landscape Trees

The fir trees are painted using the stippling method described in *Painting Techniques*. Load a liner brush with Real Brown. Beginning at the top of each tree, paint the trunk. With a filbert brush, pick up Sap Green and pounce the branches in a back and forth motion creating a triangular shape as you paint.

Pounce Fresh Foliage on some of the branches to highlight. Add red berries to some of the trees with Alizarin Crimson. Pounce snow on the top of the pine branches with Warm White.

Paint the bare-branched tree Real Brown.

Detail of medallion on five-inch doll.

Detail of medallion on four-inch doll.

Shade with Licorice. Pounce snow on some of the branches with Warm White.

Christmas Tree

Paint the Christmas tree (in the picture window on the largest doll) as you painted the landscape trees. Add tiny dots with Lemonade, Alizarin Crimson and Warm White to create lights. Allow to dry, then paint the window slats with Real Brown.

Tiny Snowman

Paint the tiny snowman on the largest doll Wicker White. Paint the hat Sap Green and scarf Alizarin Crimson. Paint two small dots for the eyes and several small dots for the mouth with Licorice. Add three buttons on the snowman's belly with Licorice. Add the arms with Real Brown.

Bridge

Paint the bridge Light Gray. Add slats on the bridge with a mix of Light Gray and Licorice. Paint the rails Wrought Iron. Pounce snow on the top of the rails with Warm White.

Fence

Paint the fence Real Brown. Add a thin line of Licorice on the left side of each slat. Pounce snow on the top of the fence rails with Warm White.

Add Sparkle

Allow the designs on the medallions to dry. Add evenly spaced dots around each medallion with Warm White.

Float a thin layer of Craft Twinkles Gold randomly on the top of the mountains, on the snow covered fields, on the rooftops, on some of the pine trees, and in the center of the rivers to suggest moonlight highlighting the various surfaces. Add small touches of Craft Twinkles Gold on the Christmas tree in the picture window.

Detail of medallion on three-inch doll.

Scarf Design

Float a layer of Craft Twinkles Gold on the scarf of the four largest dolls and the crown of the smallest one. Let dry.

Transfer or draw the pattern for the scarf on each doll. Paint the lace pattern around each doll's face with Warm White. Add the snowflakes with Warm White. Add randomly placed groupings of three dots throughout the scarf.

Add the tassel trim to the bottom of the scarf with Splendid Gold. Add dots in Warm White where the lace intersects with the scarf.

Faces

Transfer or draw the face on each doll. Paint the hair with two coats of Burnt Sienna. Add streaks to the hair with Real Brown.

Base the eyes Warm White mixed with a touch of Porcelain Blue. Shadow the top of each eye with a mix of Light Flesh and Medium Flesh. Outline the top and bottom of each eye with Real Brown.

Paint the irises Porcelain Blue and the pupils Licorice. Add a tiny dot of Warm White to the upper right corner of each iris. Paint the eyelashes and eyebrows using Real Brown. Paint two small dashes for the nose with Real Brown.

Paint the lips Alizarin Crimson. Draw a thin line with Licorice to delineate the top and bottom lip. Add a highlight with Warm White on the lower lip. Add a touch of blush on the cheeks with a mix of Medium Flesh and Rose Pink.

Completing your Dolls
Follow the directions in *General Instructions* for varnishing your dolls.

Winter Maiden can easily be painted on a larger nesting doll. This design was created on an 8-inch, 7-piece doll. You can use the same basic medallion designs for the dolls. Just add a few more buildings and trees to the medallions of the two largest dolls. You can paint the smallest doll as a maiden or change it to a snowman.

Pattern for Winter Maiden

Pattern may be hand traced or photocopied for personal use only. Pattern shown is for the six-inch doll. To obtain the pattern for each subsequent doll, copy the image at 75% on a photocopier. For example, the 4 and 1/2 inch doll's pattern will be 75% of the original design. The next doll's pattern will be 75% of that and so on.

Pattern for Winter Maiden

To obtain the correct size for each medallion, reduce each image to 75% on a photocopier.

Pattern may be hand traced or photocopied for personal use only.

Cathedral Maiden

 Painting Cathedral Maiden will be a labor of love. But I encourage you to take the time to paint it. Decorate each doll one at a time, and before you know it, you will have a wonderful work of art that you can display proudly.

Palette
FolkArt® Acrylic Paints
- Alizarin Crimson
- Burnt Sienna
- Cobalt Blue
- Gems Platinum
- Gems Ruby
- Hauser Green Light
- Hauser Green Medium
- Italian Sage
- Licorice
- Light Flesh
- Light Gray
- Medium Flesh
- Real Brown
- Rose Garden
- Rose Pink
- Sap Green
- Warm White

Delta Ceramcoat® Acrylic Paints
- Cardinal Red

DecoArt® Metallics
- Emperor's Gold
- Ice Blue
- White Pearl

Painting Surface
8-inch, 7-piece Blank Wooden Nesting Doll.

Brushes and Other Supplies
- Flat sizes #2, #4, #6, and #8
- Filbert sizes #1, #2 and #4
- Round sizes #3/10, #1 and #2
- Liner size #20/0 and #10/0
- Glaze brush 1/2"
- Masterson Sta-Wet Palette
- Water Basin
- Sanding Paper and Sponge
- Circle and Oval Templates
- DecoArt® Dura Clear Varnish Gloss

Preparation
Follow the directions in *General Instructions* to prepare your dolls for painting. Using the template, draw the face on each doll. Faces sizes for the 7-piece set are as follows: 3 inches for the largest doll, followed by 2 inches, 1 3/4 inches, 1 1/4 inches, 1 inch, 1/2 inch and 3/8 inch.

Transfer or draw the outline for each doll's scarf, medallion and crown. As you paint, refer to the color photographs of the dolls.

Paint the Background
Paint the doll faces Light Flesh. Paint the scarf of the six largest dolls Sap Green and the dress Italian Sage. Paint the crown Emperor's Gold.

Mix Cobalt Blue and Warm White to create a

soft blue color and paint the medallions. Add soft wispy clouds with Warm White on the top half of the medallions.

The smallest doll is painted Sap Green with the crown Emperor's Gold. Let dry.

Medallion Designs

Transfer the designs onto each medallion. Paint the medallions according to the instructions below for each doll.

St. Basil's Cathedral (8-inch doll)

Create a soft coral color by mixing Warm White with a touch of Alizarin Crimson and Rose Pink. Use this color to paint the cathedral, excluding the spires.

Paint the spire on the tallest tower Emperor's Gold. Outline with thinned Licorice.

Starting on the left side of the cathedral, paint the first spire Emperor's Gold. Paint the stripes Hauser Green Medium.

Detail of medallion on eight-inch doll.

cathedral with Hauser Green Medium and Warm White. Shade some of the windows with Burnt Sienna.

Paint a "V" for each bird with Light Gray. Add a stroke with Licorice on the bottom of each bird's wings.

Kazan Cathedral (7-inch doll)

Paint the main walls of the church Rose Garden. Paint the roofs Hauser Green Medium and the trim Warm White. Outline each detail of the church with thinned Licorice.

Paint the main spire and the crosses Emperor's Gold. Paint the windows on the main tower Licorice. Add a trim of Emperor's Gold to these windows. Paint the left spire Hauser Green Medium.

Paint the second spire Cardinal Red. Add a float of Gems Ruby to the spire. Add stripes with Hauser Green Medium.

Paint the third spire Warm White. Add a float of White Pearl. Paint the stripes Ice Blue.

The spires on the right are painted Emperor's Gold and Cardinal Red. Paint the pattern on the gold spire with Hauser Green Medium. Add a float of Gems Ruby to the red spire. Paint the dot patterns Ice Blue.

Paint the crosses on each spire Emperor's Gold. Add a stroke of Licorice on the left and bottom of each cross.

Following the design, paint the details on the

Detail of medallion on seven-inch doll.

The medium-sized window in the middle of the cathedral is painted Emperor's Gold. Add a float of Gems Ruby. The small windows on each side of this center window are painted Ice Blue.

Detail of medallion on six-inch doll.

The three windows on the bottom are painted Cobalt Blue. Add a float of Gems Platinum to each window. Add the details with Licorice.

Paint the birds as described above.

St. Nicholas Naval Cathedral (6-inch doll)
Paint the main walls of the cathedral with a mix of Cobalt Blue and Warm White. Make sure the mix is darker than what you used for the sky. Add the trim with Warm White.

The top windows are painted Ice Blue. The bottom windows are Emperor's Gold and trimmed with Ice Blue. Add a float of Gems Platinum to all windows.

The spires and crosses are painted Emperor's Gold. Outline the details of the building with Light Gray.

Paint the birds as described above.

Remaining Dolls
Follow the instructions for painting St. Basil's Cathedral to paint the spires on the next three dolls. The smallest doll is painted with a single rose using the instructions below for painting the roses on the scarf.

Medallion Lace
After you finish painting the designs on the medallions, add the cross-hatching lace pattern around each medallion with thinned Warm White. Add the cross-hatching pattern on the bottom rim of the largest doll with thinned Warm White

Scarf
Transfer the rose pattern to the scarf. The leaves are painted with a mix of Hauser Green Medium and Hauser Green Light. The roses are painted with a mix of Alizarin Crimson, Rose Garden and a bit of Warm White. Outline the leaves with Emperor's Gold and the roses with Warm White. Add tendrils and dots with Emperor's Gold.

Following the pattern, paint the cross-hatching on the bottom of the scarf.

Gold Crown
The gold crown is decorated with a delicate

lace pattern. Using the pattern provided as a guide, paint the lace on the crown with Warm White.

Faces

Transfer or draw the face on each doll. Paint the hair Burnt Sienna. Add details with Real Brown.

Base the eyes Warm White with a touch of Cobalt Blue. Shadow the top lid of each eye with a mix of Light Flesh and Medium Flesh. Outline the top of the eye Real Brown and the bottom of the eye Burnt Sienna.

Paint the irises Hauser Green Light and the pupils Licorice. Add a tiny dot of Warm White to the upper right corner of each iris. Paint the eyelashes and eyebrows using Real Brown.

Lace Pattern

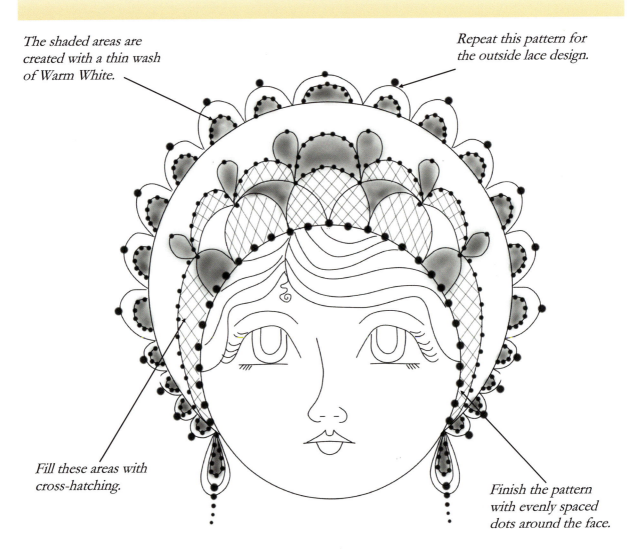

The shaded areas are created with a thin wash of Warm White.

Repeat this pattern for the outside lace design.

Fill these areas with cross-hatching.

Finish the pattern with evenly spaced dots around the face.

Outline the nose with a mix of Light Flesh and Rose Pink. Add two small dots with Real Brown.

Paint the lips Alizarin Crimson. Draw a thin line with Licorice to delineate the top and bottom lip. Add a highlight with Warm White on the lower lip. Add a touch of blush on the cheeks with a mix of Light Flesh and Rose Garden.

Completing your Dolls

Follow the directions in *General Instructions* for varnishing your dolls.

Pattern for Cathedral Maiden

Pattern may be hand traced or photocopied for personal use only. Pattern shown is for the eight-inch doll. To obtain the pattern for each subsequent doll, copy the image at 75% on a photocopier.

Pattern for Cathedral Maiden

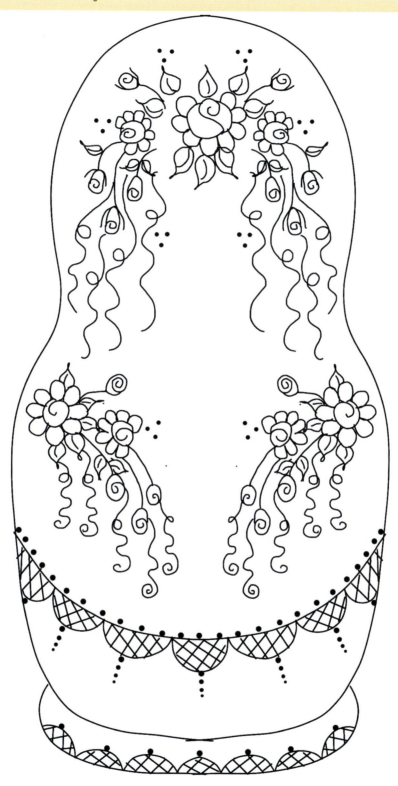

Pattern may be hand traced or photocopied for personal use only. Pattern shown is for the eight-inch doll. To obtain the pattern for each subsequent doll, copy the image at 75% on a photocopier.

Pattern for Cathedral Maiden

Pattern may be hand traced or photocopied for personal use only. To obtain the correct size for each medallion, reduce each image to 75% on a photocopier.

Pattern for Cathedral Maiden

Pattern may be hand traced or photocopied for personal use only. To obtain the correct size for each medallion, reduce each image to 75% on a photocopier.

Khokhloma Maiden

Khokhloma is the name of a Russian folk art painting style known for its red and gold colors over a black background. I created this design for a larger nesting doll set with 10-pieces, but the design can easily be adapted for a five-or eight-piece blank nesting doll.

Palette

Delta Ceramcoat® Acrylic Paints
- Autumn Brown
- Black
- Light Foliage Green
- Napthol Red Light
- Light Flesh
- Medium Flesh
- Warm White

DecoArt® Metallics
- Emperor's Gold

FolkArt® Acrylic Paints
- Alizarin Crimson
- Gems Gold
- Porcelain Blue
- Real Brown
- Rose Garden

Painting Surface
10-inch, 10-piece Blank Wooden Nesting Doll.

Brushes and Other Supplies
- Flat sizes #2, #4, #6, and #8
- Filbert sizes #1, #2 and #4
- Round sizes #3/10, #1 and #2
- Liner size #20/0 and #10/0
- Glaze brush 1/2"
- Masterson Sta-Wet Palette
- Water Basin
- Sanding Paper and Sponge
- Circle and Oval Templates
- DecoArt® Dura Clear Varnish Gloss

Preparation

Follow the directions in *General Instructions* to prepare your dolls for painting. Using the template, draw the face on each doll.

If you are painting on a 10-inch, 10-piece set, the dimensions for the faces of the ten dolls will be 3 inches, followed by 2 1/2 inches, 2 inches, 1 1/2 inches, 1 1/4 inches, 1 inch, 3/4 inch, 1/2 inch, 3/8 inch and 3/16 inch.

These measurements, however, are approximate. Since nesting dolls are hand carved, their sizes will vary and your largest doll can range anywhere from 9 3/4 to 10 1/4 inches in size. Each doll's face, therefore, should be about 1/3 the overall size of the doll.

Transfer or draw the outline for each doll's scarf, medallion and crown. As you paint, refer to the color photographs of the dolls.

Paint the Background

Paint the doll faces Light Flesh. Paint the

scarf of the six largest dolls Black and the medallion and dress Napthol Red Light. The next three dolls are painted all in black with the medallion painted in Naphtol Red Light. The smallest doll is painted Black.

Paint the band on the front of the crown of the eight largest dolls, Napthol Red Light and the rest of the crown Emperor's Gold. Paint the crown on the next doll Emperor's Gold. The smallest doll does not have a gold crown.

Allow the dolls to dry.

Medallion Design

Transfer the designs onto each medallion. The six largest dolls have golden birds on the medallion, the next three a golden flower and the smallest one just a dot daisy on its belly. The birds and flowers are painted Emperor's Gold. Emperor's Gold is a very transparent color and since you are applying it over a red and black background, you will need to apply at least three coats of paint to obtain adequate coverage.

With thinned Black, outline each bird and add the details to the face and body. Do the same for the gold flowers on the medallions of the

next three dolls. Paint the leaves of the flowers Light Foliage Green. Outline the leaves with thinned Black.

Randomly place dot daisies within the medallions of the six largest dolls. These daisies have a center dot of Emperor's Gold surrounded by five dots of Warm White. Add the dot daisy on the belly of the smallest doll.

Outline the medallion of the first eight dolls with a band of Emperor's Gold. With Warm White, paint two rows of C-strokes around the medallions of the seven largest dolls. Add dots in Warm White.

Paint one row of C-strokes around the medallion of the eighth doll along with the dots. Outline the medallion of the ninth doll with Warm White dots.

Scarf and Dress Design

Trace or transfer the flower designs and C-stroke trim to the scarf and dress of the eight largest dolls. The six largest dolls have an ornamental flower at the top of the scarf, with smaller daisies randomly placed on the rest of the scarf.

The next two dolls have a daisy on the top of the scarf surrounded by randomly placed dot daisies. The scarves of the two smallest dolls are decorated with randomly placed dot daisies.

Paint all the flowers with several coats of Emperor's Gold. Paint the leaves Light Foliage Green. Add the details for the ornamental flowers with thinned Black and thinned Napthol Red Light. Place dots of Light Foliage Green around the ornamental flowers.

Add details to the daisies on the scarf and dress with thinned Black. Paint small golden swirls extending from some of the daisies and add small dots with Warm White at the top of each swirl.

Add random dot daisies throughout the scarf. The daisies have a center dot of Emperor's Gold surrounded by five dots of Warm White. On the bottom of the dress of the six largest dolls, add gold swirls. Add a dot in Black in the center of each swirl.

Paint the C-stroke trim on the scarf with Warm White and Emperor's Gold. Add dots with Warm White.

Crown

Float a layer of Gems Gold on the crown of each doll. Add dots in Warm White to the outside and inside edge of the gold portion of the crown on the eight largest dolls. Connect the dots on the inside portion with C-strokes Add dots in Emperor's Gold around the outside edge of the red part of the crown. Fill in the crown with dot daisies. These daisies have a center of Naphtol Red Light surrounded with five dots of Warm White.

The crown on the ninth doll has a row of Warm White dots on the outside edge. The smallest doll has a crown of Warm White dots.

Create the earrings with decreasing dots in Warm White.

Faces

Transfer or draw the face on each doll. Paint the hair Autumn Brown. Add details with Black.

Base the eyes Warm White mixed with a touch of Porcelain Blue Shadow the top of each eye with a mix of Light Flesh and Medium Flesh. Outline the top and bottom of the eye Real Brown

Paint the irises Light Foliage Green and the pupils Black. Add a thin stroke with Emperor's Gold on the left bottom of each iris. Add a tiny dot of Warm White to the upper right corner of each iris. Paint the eyelashes and eyebrows using Real Brown.

Outline the nose with a mix of Light Flesh and Rose Garden. Add two small dots at the tip of the nose with Real Brown.

Paint the lips Alizarin Crimson. Draw a thin line with Black to delineate the top and bottom lip. Add a highlight with Warm White on the lower lip. Add a touch of blush on the cheeks with a mix of Light Flesh and Rose Garden.

Completing your Dolls

Follow the directions in *General Instructions* for varnishing your dolls.

Pattern for Kohkhloma Maiden

Pattern may be hand traced or photocopied for personal use only. Pattern shown is for the eight-inch doll. To obtain the pattern for the 10-inch doll, copy the image at 125% on a photocopier. To obtain the pattern for each subsequent doll, copy the image at 75%.

Pattern for Kohkhloma Maiden

Pattern may be hand traced or photocopied for personal use only. Pattern shown is for the eight-inch doll. To obtain the pattern for the 10-inch doll, copy the image at 125% on a photocopier. To obtain the pattern for each subsequent doll, copy the image at 75%.

Wild Rose Maiden

Wild Rose Maiden will make a wonderful decoration for your home. The design is painted on a 10-piece blank nesting doll, but it can easily be adapted for a five-piece or eight-piece blank nesting doll.

Palette

Delta Ceramcoat® Acrylic Paints
- Black
- Black Cherry
- Candy Bar Brown
- Light Chocolate
- Light Foliage Green
- Light Flesh
- Medium Flesh
- White

DecoArt® Metallics
- Emperor's Gold

FolkArt® Acrylic Paints
- Gems Gold
- Porcelain Blue
- Rose Garden
- Rose White
- Sap Green
- Sunflower
- Warm White

Painting Surface

10-inch, 10-piece Blank Wooden Nesting Doll.

Brushes and Other Supplies

- Flat sizes #2, #4, #6, and #8
- Filbert sizes #1, #2 and #4
- Round sizes #3/10, #1 and #2
- Liner size #20/0 and #10/0
- Glaze brush 1/2"
- Masterson Sta-Wet Palette
- Water Basin
- Sanding Paper and Sponge
- Circle and Oval Templates
- DecoArt® Dura Clear Varnish Gloss

Preparation

Follow the directions in *General Instructions* to prepare your dolls for painting. Using the template, draw the face on each doll.

If you are painting on a 10-inch, 10-piece set, the dimensions for the faces of the ten dolls will be 3 inches, followed by 2 1/2 inches, 2 inches, 1 1/2 inches, 1 1/4 inches, 1 inch, 3/4 inch, 1/2 inch, 3/8 inch and 3/16 inch.

These measurements, however, are approximate. Since nesting dolls are hand carved, their sizes will vary and your largest doll can range anywhere from 9 3/4 to 10 1/4 inches in size. Each doll's face, therefore, should be about 1/3 the overall size of the doll.

Transfer or draw the outline for each doll's scarf, medallion, apron and crown. As you paint, refer to the color photographs of the dolls.

Paint the Background

Paint the doll faces Light Flesh. For the nine largest dolls, paint the scarf Sap Green. Paint the dress Light Foliage Green. Paint the medallion Rose White. Paint the crown and the band around the middle of the scarf Emperor's Gold.

The smallest doll is painted Sap Green with a crown in Emperor's Gold. Allow the dolls to dry.

Medallion Design

Trace or transfer the designs onto each medallion. Paint the leaves with a brush mix of Sap Green and Light Foliage Green. Paint a vein down the center of the larger leaves with Sunflower.

Base the rose petals Rose Garden. While the paint is still wet, add Rose White to the top third of each rose. Blend softly. Add thin strokes with Black Cherry from the center to about halfway up the petal. Repeat with Rose White.

Double load a small brush with Sunflower and Light Chocolate. Pounce the colors on the center of each rose. Let dry. Add small dots along the outside of each rose's center with Sunflower, Light Chocolate and White.

Outline each rose petal with thinned Rose White.

Paint small daisies around the rose design. These daisies have a center dot of Sunflower surrounded by five dots of Black Cherry.

Outline the bottom of the medallions with a row of C-strokes in White. Add a second row of C-strokes with Emperor's Gold, followed by another row of White. Add dots in Emperor's Gold.

Paint dots of decreasing size along the top of the medallion.

Create the pendant necklace by painting an oval shaped jewel surrounded by small dots in White.

Apron Design

Outline the bottom of the apron with White. The lace design is created using C-strokes, cross-hatching and dots in White.

Paint evenly spaced dot daisies in the apron. These daisies have a center dot of Sunflower surrounded by five dots of White.

Scarf Design

Fill the scarf with randomly placed groupings of three dots in Emperor's Gold.

Create the lace in the gold band around the bottom of the scarf with White using C-strokes, cross-hatching and dots.

Skirt Design

Create the scroll design on the bottom of the scarf with Emperor's Gold. Finish the scroll design with evenly spaced dots in Emperor's Gold.

Fill the rest of the skirt with randomly placed groupings of three dots in Emperor's Gold. .

Create the design on the bottom of the skirt with C-strokes, cross-hatching and dots in White.

Crown

Float a layer of Gems Gold on the crown. Create the lace around the outside edge of the crown with a row of C-strokes in White, followed by a second row with Emperor's Gold, and a third row of White. Add dots on the outside and inside edge of the crown in White.

The smallest doll's crown is decorated with a row of evenly spaced dots in White around both the outside and inside edges.

Create the dangling earrings with a row of decreasing dots in White.

Faces

Transfer or draw the face on each doll. Paint the hair Candy Bar Brown. Add details with Black.

Base the eyes Warm White mixed with a touch of Porcelain Blue. Shadow the top of each eye with a mix of Light Flesh and Medium Flesh. Outline the top and bottom of the eye with Candy Bar Brown.

Paint the irises Light Foliage Green and the pupils Black. Add a thin stroke with Emperor's Gold on the left bottom of each iris. Add a tiny dot of Warm White to the upper right corner of each iris. Paint the eyelashes and eyebrows using Candy Bar Brown.

Outline the nose with a mix of Light Flesh and Rose Garden. Add two small dots at the tip of the nose with Real Brown.

Paint the lips Black Cherry. Draw a thin line with Black to delineate the top and bottom lip. Add a highlight with Warm White on the lower lip. Add a touch of blush on the cheeks with a mix of Light Flesh and Rose Garden.

Completing your Dolls

Follow the directions in *General Instructions* for varnishing your dolls.

Pattern for Wild Rose Maiden

Pattern may be hand traced or photocopied for personal use only. Pattern shown is for the eight-inch doll. To obtain the pattern for the 10-inch doll, copy the image at 125% on a photocopier. To obtain the pattern for each subsequent doll, copy the image at 75%.

Pattern for Wild Rose Maiden

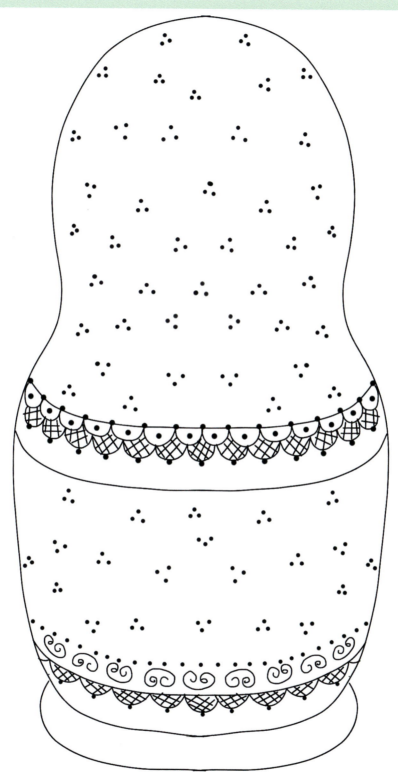

Pattern may be hand traced or photocopied for personal use only. Pattern shown is for the eight-inch doll. To obtain the pattern for the 10-inch doll, copy the image at 125% on a photocopier. To obtain the pattern for each subsequent doll, copy the image at 75%.

CPSIA information can be obtained at www.ICGtesting.com
Printed in the USA
LVIW01n1813070916
503619LV00006B/22